BIGGEST NAMES IN SPORTS

GERRIT COLE

BASEBALL STAR

by Hubert Walker

FOCUS READERS.

NAVIGATOR

WWW.FOCUSREADERS.COM

Focus Readers is distributed by North Star Editions:
sales@northstareditions.com | 888-417-0195

Produced for Focus Readers by Red Line Editorial.

Photographs ©: Alex Brandon/AP Images, cover, 1; Jeff Roberson/AP Images, 4–5; Kyodo/AP Images, 7; Patrick Semansky/AP Images, 9; Rick Loomis/Los Angeles Times/Getty Images, 10–11; John S Peterson/Icon SMI/Newscom, 13; Cliff Welch/Icon SMI/Newscom, 15; Keith Srakocic/AP Images, 16–17; Justin Berl/Icon Sportswire, 19; Shutterstock Images, 21; Eric Christian Smith/AP Images, 22–23; Michael Wyke/AP Images, 25; Kathy Willens/AP Images, 27; Red Line Editorial, 29

Library of Congress Cataloging-in-Publication Data
Names: Walker, Hubert, author.
Title: Gerrit Cole : baseball star / by Hubert Walker.
Description: Lake Elmo, MN : Focus Readers, [2021] | Series: Biggest names in sports | Includes index. | Audience: Grades 4-6
Identifiers: LCCN 2020036711 (print) | LCCN 2020036712 (ebook) | ISBN 9781644936986 (hardcover) | ISBN 9781644937341 (paperback) | ISBN 9781644938065 (pdf) | ISBN 9781644937709 (ebook)
Subjects: LCSH: Cole, Gerrit, 1990---Juvenile literature. | Pitchers--United States--Biography--Juvenile literature. | Baseball players--United States--Biography--Juvenile literature.
Classification: LCC GV865.C642 W35 2021 (print) | LCC GV865.C642 (ebook) | DDC 796.357092 [B]--dc23
LC record available at https://lccn.loc.gov/2020036711
LC ebook record available at https://lccn.loc.gov/2020036712

Printed in the United States of America
Mankato, MN
012021

ABOUT THE AUTHOR

Hubert Walker enjoys running, hunting, and going to the dog park with his best pal. He grew up in Georgia but moved to Minnesota in 2018. Overall, he loves his new home, but he's not a fan of the cold winters.

TABLE OF CONTENTS

CHAPTER 1

WORLD SERIES ACE

Gerrit Cole stood on the mound in Game 5 of the 2019 World Series. He and the Houston Astros were facing the Washington Nationals. The Astros held a 2–0 lead in the bottom of the second inning. But Cole was in trouble. The Nationals had runners on first and third with nobody out.

Gerrit Cole hurls a pitch during his Game 5 start in the 2019 World Series.

Washington batter Ryan Zimmerman had one ball and two strikes. On the next pitch, Cole threw a wicked **slider**. Zimmerman swung, but he wasn't even close. Cole had struck him out.

However, Cole couldn't relax yet. He still needed two more outs to end the inning. Victor Robles came to the plate next. Cole's first two pitches were strikes. On the third pitch, Robles hit a ground ball directly to the shortstop. The shortstop tossed the ball to the second baseman for one out. The second baseman quickly threw it to first base for a **double play**. Cole had gotten out of a major jam, and the Astros still led 2–0.

CHAPTER 3

IN THE MAJORS, ON THE MOUND

Gerrit Cole made his major league **debut** in June 2013. On the first pitch of his MLB career, he threw a fastball for a strike. On his second pitch, he threw another hard fastball. It was strike two. Then Cole threw a third fastball across the plate. The batter had no chance. He struck out swinging. All three pitches

In 2013, approximately half of all Cole's pitches were fastballs.

had gone 96 miles per hour (154 km/h). Pirates fans roared in appreciation.

Cole didn't stop there. At one point in the game, he retired 13 batters in a row. He pitched into the seventh inning and allowed only two runs. He didn't walk a single batter. It was an impressive start for the 22-year-old **rookie**.

BATTER UP

Like most pitchers, Cole is not a good hitter. But his first major league at-bat was one to remember. The bases were loaded in the second inning. Cole had three balls and two strikes. On the next pitch, Cole lined a single to center field. Two runners scored on the play. Cole's hit gave the Pirates a 2–0 lead.

Cole pitches to a San Francisco Giants batter during a
May 2014 game.

Cole had always been great at throwing
fastballs. But he knew he needed to work
on other pitches. In 2014, Cole improved
his curveball. A curveball is much slower

than a fastball. The ball moves downward as it approaches the batter. Cole's hard work paid off. With a greater variety of pitches, he was able to keep batters guessing.

In 2015, Cole had his best season yet. He racked up 19 wins and led the Pirates to their best record in years. He was also named to the All-Star team for the first time in his career. However, the season ended on a sour note. Pittsburgh faced the Chicago Cubs in the Wild Card Game. Cole gave up four runs in a losing effort.

Cole had a rough year in 2016. He dealt with injuries for much of the season. He posted a disappointing 7–10 record.

Cole delivers a pitch during a 2017 game against the Arizona Diamondbacks.

Cole stayed healthy in 2017, but he still struggled on the mound. He allowed more runs than usual, and he gave up more walks. If Cole was going to regain his All-Star status, something had to change.

CHAPTER 4

HUGE IMPROVEMENTS

In January 2018, Gerrit Cole received an unexpected phone call. He learned that the Pirates had traded him to the Houston Astros. Cole felt surprised but happy about the trade. The Astros were an excellent team, and Cole knew he would have a good chance at winning a World Series title.

Cole celebrates after striking out a batter during his second start with the Houston Astros in 2018.

Cole's team wasn't the only thing that changed in 2018. He also made some pitching adjustments. For example, he started throwing more pitches to the top of the **strike zone**. Thanks to that change, Cole made more batters miss.

In addition, Cole improved his changeup. This pitch is meant to fool batters. When it travels toward the plate, it looks similar to a fastball. However, the ball moves much slower. As a result, batters swing too early.

These changes took Cole's pitching to another level. In 2018, he made the All-Star team for the second time in his career. He also totaled 276 strikeouts.

Cole waves to Astros fans after posting his
300th strikeout of the 2019 season.

Very few pitchers in MLB history have
recorded 300 strikeouts in a season. But
in 2019, Cole had his best season yet. He
totaled 326 strikeouts that year. He also
recorded 19 straight wins.

Despite two incredible years with
Houston, Cole's dreams of a World Series

title didn't come true. And after the 2019 season ended, so did his contract with the Astros. Cole was free to sign with any team. The New York Yankees offered him a massive nine-year deal. Cole was thrilled to join his favorite team.

Yankees fans had to wait longer than expected to see Cole in pinstripes. As

FIGHTING THE VIRUS

COVID-19 hit New York especially hard. In response, Cole decided to help out. He made a large donation to a charity called Direct Relief. This group assists doctors, nurses, and other health-care workers. It gives them protective equipment such as masks and gloves. These tools make it less likely that workers will get the virus.

Cole began the 2020 season strong by winning his first three starts.

the 2020 season was about to start, the COVID-19 virus hit the United States. As a result, MLB shortened the season. Finally, in July 2020, it was time to play ball. Cole was able to pitch for the Yankees at last.

GERRIT COLE

- Height: 6 feet 4 inches (193 cm)
- Weight: 225 pounds (102 kg)
- Birth date: September 8, 1990
- Hometown: Orange, California
- High school: Orange Lutheran High School (Orange, California)
- College: University of California, Los Angeles (2008–2011)
- Minor league teams: Bradenton Marauders (2012); Indianapolis Indians (2012–2013)
- MLB teams: Pittsburgh Pirates (2013–2017); Houston Astros (2018–2019); New York Yankees (2020–)
- Major awards: MLB All-Star (2015, 2018, 2019); MLB strikeout leader (2019)

Pittsburgh

New York

Los Angeles

Indianapolis

Orange

Houston

Bradenton

FOCUS ON
GERRIT COLE

Write your answers on a separate piece of paper.

1. Write a paragraph that explains the main ideas of Chapter 2.

2. Do you think Cole should have joined the Yankees after he finished high school? Why or why not?

3. Which team did Cole join in 2018?
> **A.** Pittsburgh Pirates
> **B.** Houston Astros
> **C.** New York Yankees

4. What would most likely happen if Cole threw a fastball on every pitch?
> **A.** He would get more batters out because the fastball is his best pitch.
> **B.** He would be able to pitch more innings because fastballs take less effort.
> **C.** He wouldn't get as many batters out because they would know what to expect.

Answer key on page 32.

GLOSSARY

debut
First appearance.

double play
When a team records two outs on the same play.

draft
A system that allows teams to acquire new players coming into a league.

farm system
A group of minor league teams that help players develop their skills. Each MLB team has its own farm system. Good players usually move up to higher levels in the system.

rookie
A professional athlete in his or her first year.

scouts
People who look for talented young players.

slider
A pitch that moves down and away from the batter.

strike zone
The area over home plate that is above the batter's knees and below the batter's shoulders.

TO LEARN MORE

BOOKS

Savage, Jeff. *Baseball Super Stats*. Minneapolis: Lerner Publications, 2018.

Velasco, Catherine Ann. *Behind the Scenes of Pro Baseball*. North Mankato, MN: Capstone Press, 2019.

Ventura, Marne. *STEM in Baseball*. Minneapolis: Abdo Publishing, 2018.

NOTE TO EDUCATORS

Visit **www.focusreaders.com** to find lesson plans, activities, links, and other resources related to this title.

INDEX